The Ivy Hero

The Brave Life of Sergeant William Shemin

The Ivy Hero

The Brave Life of Sergeant William Shemin

Sara Shemin Cass and Dan Burstein

Illustrations by Gary Bullock

CITY POINT PRESS

FIRST EDITION

Published by City Point Press
www.citypointpress.com

For sales inquiries, contact Simon & Schuster (866) 506-1949
For rights inquiries, contact City Point Press (203) 571-0781
For author inquiries, visit www.theivyhero.com

Paperback ISBN: 978-1-947951-64-8

eBook ISBN: 978-1-947951-65-5

Manufactured in Canada

TO ELSIE—
the matriarch of the Shemin family—
AND TO INA, EMANUEL (father to Sara) AND
LEON BURSTEIN (father to Dan),
all of whom embody the Shemin spirit,
and to all the children, grandchildren, and generations
yet to come of the extended Shemin family,
who inspired us to write this book.

Contents

OPPOSITE: *Ceremony naming the William Shemin Midtown Community School in honor of Sgt. William Shemin, November, 2019.*

Preface

Welcome to *The Ivy Hero*, the true story of Sergeant William (Bill) Shemin. Our tale will take you back in time over one hundred years and all the way up to present day. Bill Shemin is the grandfather of one of the authors of this book (Sara) and was the first cousin of the grandmother of the other author (Dan).

Bill Shemin was an American soldier who fought in World War I. He was dedicated, fearless, and brave. As you read these pages, you will understand why he is a hero. But what about the "ivy" part?

Sergeant Shemin fought with the U.S. Army's 4th Division, which is known as the "Ivy" Division because the Roman Numeral for 4 is composed of an I before a V—IV—so its nickname is "IVY." But there's a more poetic reason as well. The Ivy Division's motto, mirroring the way the ivy plant itself grows, is "steadfast and loyal." After serving in World War I in the Ivy Division, Bill Shemin used the ivy plant as the logo for his tree and plant business. And "steadfast and loyal" was how he lived his life.

You will meet more than one hero in this story.

In addition to Bill, you will learn about his daughter, Elsie Shemin-Roth. She waged her own battle for many years after Sgt. Shemin's death to have the U.S. government award him the Medal of Honor that rightfully should have been awarded him at the time of his service in World War I.

You will also meet Henry Johnson, an African American soldier who, like Bill, fought bravely and heroically in World War I—not far away from the battlefields where Bill fought in France in 1918. Like Bill, Henry Johnson's bravery in saving his fellow soldiers' lives went unrecognized with a Medal of Honor in his lifetime, even though his actions certainly called for one.

Private Henry Johnson during World War I.

William Shemin was discriminated against because he was a Jewish American, and there was a pronounced mood of anti-Semitism in the United States in 1918 that is, unfortunately, once again on the rise today. Henry Johnson was discriminated against because he was African American at a time when African Americans were severely discriminated against in the U.S. Army and throughout American life.

Although much progress has been made, racial and religious discrimination have been with American society from the birth of our country to the present day. The struggle for equality and freedom continues, as people try to make the United States a "more perfect union." The pain and suffering of war and discrimination run through this story, but it has a hopeful ending. And so much can be learned from the lives and experiences of these heroes!

Before you start reading, there are a few things you should know about the design and organization of this book.

Words that are in **bold** are defined in the Glossary that appears on page 103.

Special material appearing with its own title in a box with a yellow background is a "Sidebar," and provides further insight to the main story in the book.

On page 107, you will find some questions that relate William Shemin's life experiences to those of today's young people and students—you may find these interesting to think about.

Sergeant William Shemin during World War I.

A website for this book provides more information and will be regularly updated: www.TheIvyHero.com. We invite your comments online at the website.

We hope you enjoy the story we have brought to life from our family history as much as we enjoyed writing it.

—**Sara & Dan**

Ivy is not boastful like a rose, but steadfast and sturdy.
When you try to cut it down, it simply grows back.
The beautiful emerald leaves glisten in the sun and
cover the ground with the softness of spring and
the resilience to survive the winter. No matter what,
ivy is a survivor.

—TONYA ELISHA MELE
Teacher, William Shemin
Midtown Community School

The Ivy Hero

The Brave Life of Sergeant William Shemin

Daughters Ina Shemin Bass and Elsie Shemin-Roth receiving their father's Medal of Honor from President Barack Obama at the White House on June 2, 2015.

What is a Hero?

We are a nation—a people—who remember our heroes. We take seriously our responsibility to only send them when war is necessary . . . We never forget their sacrifice. And we believe that it's never too late to say thank you.

—PRESIDENT BARACK OBAMA
Medal of Honor Ceremony for
William Shemin and Henry Johnson,
THE WHITE HOUSE, 2015

What makes a hero?

Is it someone who can save the world like Superman?

The finest heroes are ordinary men and women who do extraordinary things.

Heroes perform acts and deeds of strength and character. They inspire us!

Great military soldiers **sacrifice** everything to defend our freedom.

William "Bill" Shemin was a hero to everyone who knew him.

He was a hero on the playing field.

He was a hero in war.

He was a hero to his entire family.

In 2015, almost one hundred years after Bill Shemin bravely fought in World War I, President Barack Obama awarded him the Medal of Honor, the highest military award in the United States.

A hero can change the world and the people in it. How did William Shemin become a hero?

The Shemin family came from a small town called Orsha in what is today Belarus, near Russia. In the 1890s, this river town had a population of about 13,000.

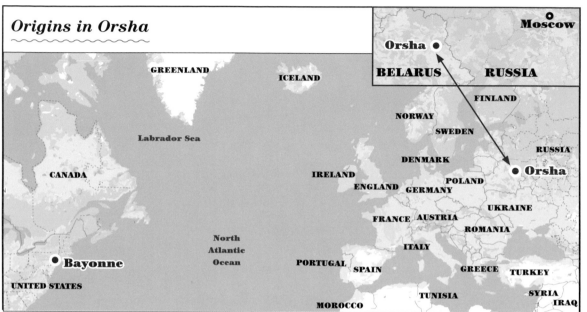

Origins in Orsha

More than half of the people who lived there were Jewish.

At that time, **ethnic** groups were being attacked for their religious beliefs. Violent attacks to destroy the Jewish people and their homes were called **pogroms**. Bill's parents fled the pogroms in search of a better life in America.

Anti-Semitic Laws in Russia

In Russia in the 1890s and early 1900s, **anti-Semitic** laws often kept Jews from owning or working the land. They also sometimes prevented Jews from getting an education. By coming to the United States, Jewish immigrants were able to find a safe place to work and make a life that was forbidden in Russia and Eastern Europe. The Shemin family believed in the values of hard work and education. Even though America was not free from anti-Semitism, the United States offered far more opportunity for newly arrived Jewish immigrants than Russia did.

18

They settled on the Lower East Side of New York City. The city was filled with **immigrants** from Russia and Europe. Jewish residents sometimes called each other "**landsman**." This was a **Yiddish** word used to describe Jewish people who came from the same places overseas and ended up living side by side in America.

In the late 1890s, Bill Shemin was the first child born on American soil to this newly arrived American family. Destined to be big and strong as a teenager and an adult, Bill was a whopping fifteen pounds at birth.

Bill at age 1.

After about a year, the family moved to Bayonne, New Jersey, which became Bill's permanent home.

Bill was the light in his parents' eyes. He was also a tough kid who loved to learn. And he was a great athlete!

Bill loved sports— *all* sports.

Bill at age 2.

Bill at age 8 with his younger sister, Min (known later as Mildred) at age 6.

*Bill as an
athlete:
wrestler,
football star,
and baseball
player for
the semipro
Bayonne
Sea Lions,
circa 1912.*

He was a long-distance swimmer. He wrestled. He boxed.

Bill convinced his parents to set up a boxing bag in the basement to practice his hooks and jabs.

Bill liked to play football. And he was good at lacrosse.

But he *loved* to play baseball.

In fact, Bill Shemin was good enough at baseball to get scouted and **recruited** for a team called the Bayonne Sea Lions at age fifteen.

They paid Bill to play.

He was just a teenager!

Bill's Competitive Nature

Growing up, Bill took great pride in his neat handwriting. However, he was always the runner-up in the annual school **penmanship** contest. Year after year, even though Bill was edged out by one girl in the class, he never gave up trying to do his best and win the award. Bill Shemin was a born **competitor**. Everyone admired his beautiful handwriting.

In his junior year of high school, Bill saw an advertisement in a magazine.

"DO YOU WANT TO BE A FOREST RANGER?"

At the age of sixteen, Bill did not know what he wanted to do with the rest of his life. Maybe he could go to school and learn how to be a forest ranger? Working outdoors appealed to his sense of adventure.

Bill applied to Ranger School and was accepted! Now he needed to convince his parents to let him leave high school early to attend this ranger program. Going to the first-ever forest ranger school training program in America was a huge **opportunity**. Would his parents let him attend?

No problem!

He persuaded them.

Once Bill got his parent's approval, he committed to going. Now he had to figure out how to travel north to get there. Ranger School was located far away in Wanakena, New York. That was a long distance from Bill's house in Bayonne, New Jersey.

No problem!

Bill boarded a train heading north. Unfortunately, the railroad tracks did not extend all the way to his **destination**. Nor was there a road all the way to camp. What would Bill do now?

No problem!

Bill climbed into a canoe and paddled! He traveled across Cranberry Lake to the New York State Ranger School in the Adirondacks, which was part of the New York State College of Forestry at Syracuse University. Once there, he met the other students living in tents. There was no heat, no running water, and only an **outhouse**. Some winter days the temperature dropped to as cold as thirty degrees below zero.

They got right to work. Some had already spent months blasting rocks and leveling the ground so they could construct their own classroom buildings and sleeping **quarters**. Bill was ready to get right to work to do anything he could to help.

Bill (3rd from right) with his Class of 1914 at The Ranger School, Wanakena, New York.

William Shemin was determined. He could paddle across a lake, construct a building, be a forest ranger— and do anything else he wanted to do! This sense of determination and willingness to do hard work at such an early age would become important qualities for his whole life.

ABOVE: *Bill in the winter at school.*

RIGHT: *Years later, William Shemin's Ranger School honored him with a plaque.*

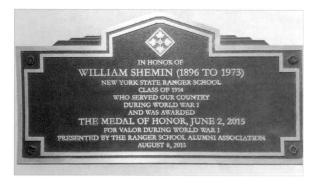

IN HONOR OF
WILLIAM SHEMIN (1896 TO 1973)
NEW YORK STATE RANGER SCHOOL
CLASS OF 1914
WHO SERVED OUR COUNTRY
DURING WORLD WAR I
AND WAS AWARDED
THE MEDAL OF HONOR, JUNE 2, 2015
FOR VALOR DURING WORLD WAR I
PRESENTED BY THE RANGER SCHOOL ALUMNI ASSOCIATION
AUGUST 8, 2015

The Great War

World War I (sometimes known in those days as "The Great War") began in 1914. In the United States, newspaper boys, also called **newsies**, barked from every corner, "Read all about it! Read all about it!" U.S. President Woodrow Wilson and the rest of America watched as World War I spread throughout Europe and millions of soldiers and civilians died.

NORWAY

SWEDEN

DENMARK

UNITED KINGDOM

NETHERLANDS

GERMANY

RUSSIA

BELGIUM
LUXEMBOURG

AUSTRO-HUNGARY

FRANCE

SWITZERLAND

ROMANIA
Joined 1915

Yellow: Allies
Pink: Central Powers
Blue: Neutral

MONTENEGRO

ITALY
Joined 1915

SERBIA

BULGARIA
Joined 1915

ALBANIA

SPAIN

PORTUGAL

GREECE   TURKEY

During World War I, two distinct **alliances** *went to war with each other. The map shows where these countries were located at that time. Some countries that fought in the war have changed their names or boundaries since then.*

World War I was being fought by more than thirty-two countries on several **continents** including Europe, Asia, and Africa. President Wilson was at first determined to keep America out of this war.

As Germans advanced into Allied territory, they plowed through Belgium and began attacking France, a country that was an important friend to America.

In 1915, a German **submarine** killed over 1,100 people on a British ship called the *Lusitania*. Britain was among America's closest friends and allies in the world. And over one hundred Americans were among the dead on the *Lusitania*. This made Americans very angry and would later contribute to the United States entering the war.

Then, in 1917, Germany abandoned its pledge to refrain from submarine attacks on American passenger and merchant ships crossing the Atlantic. Several U.S. ships were sunk after that.

With the Germans gaining ground in Europe, the future of America's friends, like Britain and France, looking worse by the day, and with shipping across the Atlantic threatened, President Wilson and the United States

Congress announced that America could no longer remain **neutral** in World War I. The United States would join the fight and stand with the Allies (see map on page 28).

American soldiers were needed on the **front lines** right away.

Bill Shemin was just a teenager, but he wanted to join them.

All across the country special **military** posters called on young people to fight to defend the U.S.A. and its allies. Songs like "Over There" encouraged young men to **enlist**. **Patriotic** tunes were played on the radio all the time.

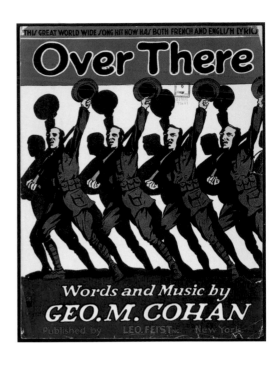

Bill Shemin felt like the songs and posters were speaking directly to him. Where could he sign up?

Bill's parents did not want Bill to go into the army. They believed their son was too young to be on the front lines of a world war. They had fled from a Russia where young men were regularly **drafted** into the **tsar**'s army. But Bill believed that because

31

America had given his family its chance to start over in a free country, now it was his **duty** to join the U.S. Army and become part of the fight. Back in Russia, so many things had been forbidden because the Shemins were Jewish. Here in America, there was freedom, safety, and the opportunity to work and raise a family. Bill wanted to fight to protect those rights that existed in his family's new country.

There was just one catch. William Shemin was still too young to be drafted. Was there any way he could convince the army to let him in? What if he decided not to tell the army his *real* age? After some arguing, Bill convinced his father to help him pretend to be older . . . just old enough to join the army. Now Bill was a can-do American, ready to fight for the red, white, and blue!

Joining the Army

October 1917

After signing up to be a soldier, Bill was sent south for training at Camp Greene in Charlotte, North Carolina. Soldiers there learned the basics of movement in the field, night operations, and route marching. They were taught how to handle a weapon and dig a **trench**. Much of the fighting in World War I was called "trench warfare" for good reason.

Private William Shemin, age 20, Camp Greene,
Charlotte, North Carolina, 1917.

November 1917–April 1918

While he was in North Carolina, Bill had the chance to use his skills from Ranger School. He helped build the **barracks**, the hospital, and the dining hall. Bill also trained to be a sharpshooter in the **infantry**.

March–August 1918

In early 1918, the Germans began the first of several spring **raids** on the **Western Front**. The German troops who had been fighting since 1914 were exhausted. But the Allies were exhausted too. The American troops that started arriving in 1917 helped refresh the fighting strength of the Alliance and were ultimately decisive in winning the war.

Bill, third from left.

More and more American troops **deployed** to Europe. In the spring of 1918, an American ship called the *USS Princess Matoika* sailed to France with a boatload of new recruits. Bill was on that ship!

Bill Joins the Second Battle of the Marne

After several months of action in France, Bill's Company G of the 47th Infantry **Regiment**, 4th Division—the one known as the "Ivy Division"—was sent to the front lines in a small French town called Bazoches, on the Vesle River. The **campaign** was a part of the ending phase of the Second Battle of the Marne, one of the most important battles in World War I where many soldiers died. The town was mostly farmland with scattered patches of forest.

A railroad ran near the town, and a battle was shaping up for the land, river, and rail line.

Soldiers on the front lines in places like Bazoches did not live in a tent or barracks. They lived in dark, wet, muddy, cold ditches called trenches. Allies hunkered down in trenches on one side of the battlefield. The Germans stayed on the other side. In a trench, a soldier was better protected from **artillery** and gunfire, and even air attack.

The area between the allied and enemy trenches was called "**no-man's-land**" because it lay between the trenches of the warring sides and held the key to pushing back one or the other and winning or losing ground in the war. No-man's-land was open space of varying size—sometimes only as wide as a football field and a half. This was land that both sides desperately fought to control.

Heroes on the Battlefield:
Bill Shemin and
Henry Johnson

Deep in the Trenches

In Bazoches, the ground smelled sour and terrible. In his trench, Bill saw gigantic rats, outbreaks of lice, and many dead bodies. Sometimes soldiers developed a condition called "**trench foot**" from standing in water and mud for so long.

Gas mask.

Stepping out of the trench into no-man's-land was worse. Troops had to survive the hail of bullets flying everywhere, the barbs of twisted wire on the ground, and the poison of deadly **mustard gas**.

At one point, the Americans in Bill's trench needed to locate a German machine gun nest. The first two soldiers were sent out to scout locations. They were killed. Now other soldiers had to run across the field and attack, even though there was a good chance they would be injured or killed, too.

Bill and the other soldiers had to make an impossible choice. Was anyone brave enough to risk certain death if they tried to rescue a fellow soldier? Or should that man stand by while his fellow soldier **perished** in the battlefield?

Which choice would Bill make?

From inside his trench in Bazoches, Bill saw a fellow soldier who had fallen a far distance away from him in an open field. Bill could see that the man was shot, but still alive. Without wasting a moment, Bill jumped from the safety of the trench and dashed towards the injured soldier.

When he got close, Bill realized he knew this soldier. The wounded man was his best friend from Newark, Jim Pritchard, who was 6 feet tall and weighed 200 pounds. On this sunny day in an open field with no cover, Bill lifted Jim and carried him back to the Allied trench. Somehow Bill was able to **dodge** bullets and **barbed wire** to carry Jim to safety.

After he rescued Jim Pritchard, Bill did something even more incredible than before. He went back into

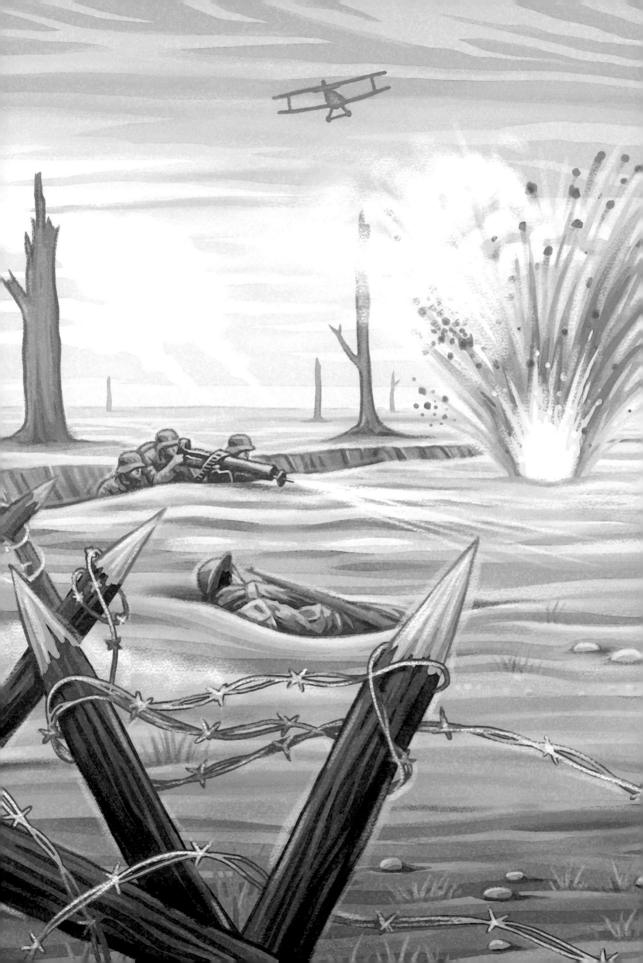

no-man's-land again, braving machine gun, small arms fire, and air bombardment. Bill repeated the bold rescue for a second soldier. Then he went back to save a third soldier!

Bill Shemin rescued not one, not two, but *three* soldiers that day, running across the football field and half length of no-man's-land under fire. Although he had made three daring rescues, Bill knew that he had more work to do. When all of Bill's senior officers were killed or suffered **casualties**, Bill reorganized and took command of the **platoon** quickly and efficiently and led everyone to safety. One lieutenant who served with Bill said he was "calm, cool, intelligent, and personally utterly fearless."

Bill believed that he was just doing his job.

Bazoches: At the End of the Second Battle of the Marne

THE BATTLE FOR BAZOCHES:
Bill's Company G, 47th Infantry Regiment, 4th Infantry Division, worked with French forces to rescue a small town in France called Bazoches.

THE WEAPONS: helmets, gas masks, rifles, and bayonets

THE OUTCOME: The Second Battle of the Marne was one of the most important battles in World War I. The Americans were able to stop the Germans from advancing. Many people died in this battle, which was fought over many months and in many locations. Bazoches was just one small **skirmish** that came at the end of this long and important battle of World War I, but it was the battle of a lifetime for William Shemin.

Bill, second from left.

Injured but Not Down

On August 9, 1918, while waging hand-to-hand combat in the ongoing fighting near Bazoches, Sergeant William Shemin was wounded and found unconscious during battle. He had pieces of broken metal from a bomb, called **shrapnel**, lodged in his back. There was also a bullet behind his ear. Doctors said it was just an inch from his brain! The bullet had apparently ricocheted off his helmet buckle, deflecting the trajectory that might have otherwise killed him. Forever after, Bill would say that buckle saved his life.

Bill's heroics had helped save the day for the Allies, but now he was seriously wounded. He spent five weeks recovering in the field hospital. It felt like forever. He missed being in the middle of the action. When the army offered him the chance to go home, he refused. Bill insisted that he was strong and tough enough to rejoin the 4th Infantry Division. Bill wanted to go where the war needed him.

Soon William Shemin would take part in one of the most important and deadliest battles of World War I, the Meuse-Argonne Offensive.

Could a group of tired Allied soldiers continue in combat with constant attacks by artillery, mustard gas, and military planes? It would not be easy.

The Allies advanced through the Argonne Forest for nearly two months. Although Bill was not even back to full strength after his August injuries and his hospital stay, he managed to play a role at Meuse-Argonne, the last Allied offensive of the war.

The battle that began in September 1918, finally ended on November 11, 1918, or what became known as Armistice Day, when the Germans finally **surrendered**. The Allied Forces were **victorious**.

Armistice Day is now celebrated in the United States as Veterans Day, a day of remembrance for soldiers from all American wars, including battles that were fought before or after World War I.

> ### *The Meuse-Argonne Offensive*
>
> The Meuse-Argonne Offensive is known as one of the largest, most important actions on the Western Front. During the offensive, over 1.2 million American soldiers (including Bill) joined with the French army to fight the remaining Central Powers. Meuse-Argonne quickly became one of the deadliest battles in American history. More than 26,000 soldiers were killed in action and over 120,000 were injured in just six weeks. Deadly as it was, it led to the end of World War I and the **armistice** of November 11, 1918.

Henry Johnson: An American Hero

During the World War I battles in France in 1918, there was another American hero who fought on a battlefield in France, not far from Bill Shemin. He was a soldier named Henry Johnson.

Henry Johnson and Bill Shemin never knew each other in life, but the two men have become linked together by history. Nearly one hundred years after both young soldiers fought hero-ically for America and the Allies on the battlefields of France, and faced different forms of discrimination, one for being Jewish and the other for being African American, both men would end up being **honored** by the United States for their bravery in World War I.

Henry Johnson being inducted into the Hall of Heroes at the Pentagon in Washington, D.C. From left to right: Robert O. Work, Deputy Secretary of Defense; Brad Carson, Under Secretary of the Army; Louis Wilson, Command Sergeant Major; Gen. Daniel Allyn, Vice Chief of Staff; Daniel A. Dailey, Sergeant Major of the Army.

Who Was Henry Johnson?

Adapted From President Barack Obama's speech awarding the
Medal of Honor to Henry Johnson posthumously (June 2, 2015)

When the United States entered World War I, Henry Johnson enlisted. He joined one of only a few units that he could: the all-Black 369th Infantry Regiment, The Harlem Hellfighters. And soon, he was headed overseas.

At the time, our military was **segregated**. Most Black soldiers served in labor battalions, not combat units. But General Pershing sent the 369th to fight with the French Army, which accepted them as their own. Quickly, the Hellfighters lived up to their name. And in the early hours of May 15, 1918, Henry Johnson became a legend.

His battalion was in Northern France, tucked into a trench. Some slept—but he couldn't. Henry and another soldier, Needham Roberts, stood **sentry** along no-man's-land. In the pre-dawn, it was pitch black, and silent. And then—a click— the sound of wire cutters.

A German raiding party—at least a dozen soldiers, maybe more— fired a hail of bullets. Henry fired back until his rifle was empty. Then he and Needham threw grenades. Both of them were hit. Needham lost consciousness. Two enemy soldiers began to carry him away while another provided cover, firing at Henry. But Henry refused to let them take his brother-in-arms. He shoved another magazine into his rifle. It jammed. He turned the gun around and swung it at one of the enemy, knocking him down. Then he grabbed the only weapon he had left— his Bolo knife—and went to rescue Needham. Henry took down one enemy soldier, then the other. The soldier he'd knocked down with his rifle recovered, and Henry was wounded again. But armed with just his knife, Henry took him down, too . . .

As the sun rose, the scale of what happened became clear. In just a few minutes of fighting, two Americans had defeated an entire raiding party. And Henry Johnson saved his fellow soldier.

Henry became one of our most famous soldiers of the war. His picture was printed on recruitment posters and ads for Victory War Stamps. Former President Teddy Roosevelt wrote that he was

Poster celebrating Henry Johnson and Needham Roberts, two African American soldiers, for their bravery in France, 1918

one of the bravest men in the war. In 1919, Henry rode triumphantly in a victory parade.

Henry was one of the first Americans to receive France's highest award for valor. But his own nation didn't award him anything . . . Nothing for his bravery, though he had saved a fellow soldier at great risk to himself. His injuries left him crippled. He couldn't find work. His marriage fell apart and in his early 30s, he passed away.

Now, America can't change what happened to Henry Johnson. We can't change what happened to too many soldiers like him, who went uncelebrated because our nation judged them by the color of their skin and not the content of their character. But we can do our best to make it right. Today, 97 years after his extraordinary acts of courage and selflessness, I'm proud to award him the Medal of Honor.

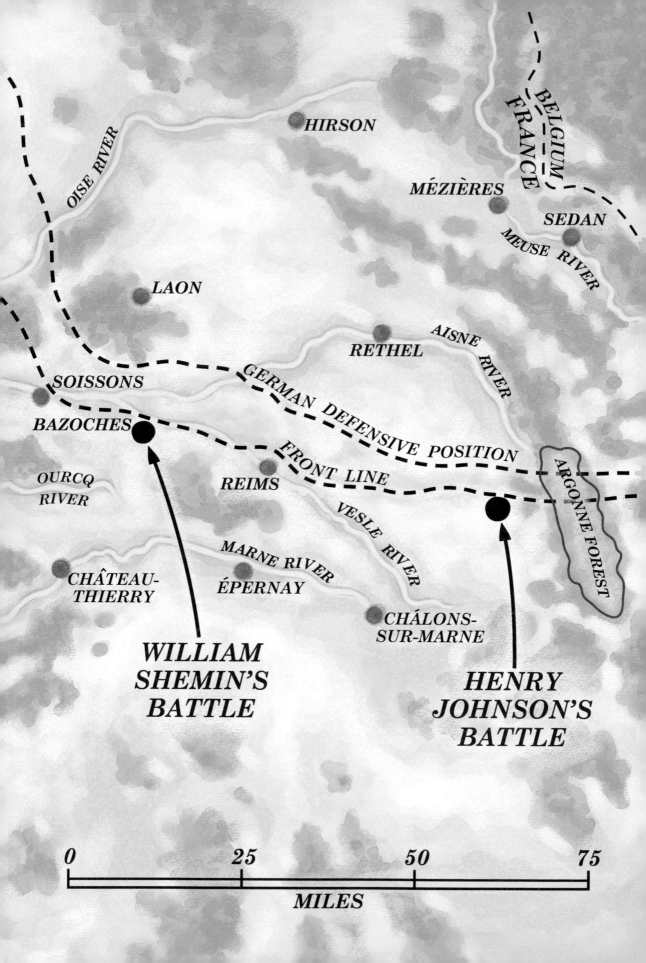

HIRSON

BELGIUM
FRANCE

MÉZIÈRES

SEDAN

OISE RIVER

MEUSE RIVER

LAON

RETHEL

AISNE RIVER

SOISSONS

GERMAN DEFENSIVE POSITION

BAZOCHES

FRONT LINE

ARGONNE FOREST

OURCQ
RIVER

REIMS

VESLE RIVER

CHÂTEAU-
THIERRY

MARNE RIVER

ÉPERNAY

CHÂLONS-
SUR-MARNE

**WILLIAM
SHEMIN'S
BATTLE**

**HENRY
JOHNSON'S
BATTLE**

0   25   50   75

MILES

OPPOSITE: *The map indicates the locations of the battle sites where William Shemin and Henry Johnson responded with acts of heroism.*

The 47th Infantry, part of the 4th Division, is shown pulling back from the front, evacuating the wounded, and resting. Sgt. Shemin is possibly somewhere in this picture.

This peaceful scene of the field in Bazoches, France, in 2018 stands in stark contrast to the battle scene 100 years earlier in 1918, when Bill rescued three of his comrades.

Army of Occupation

After the Allied victory, Bill volunteered to stay on with the Army of Occupation. In an **occupation**, a group of soldiers stay inside a defeated country to keep the peace. Bill remained in a German town called Vallendar until August 1919 when he was honorably discharged from the United States Army.

While stationed in Germany, Bill (far left) played baseball for the 47th Infantry Regimental Team of the Army of Occupation in 1919.

Bill (second row, left) in uniform while serving in the Army of Occupation.

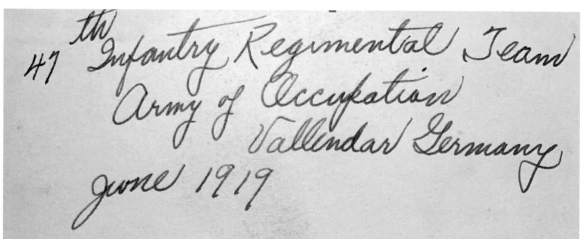

Bill, middle row, second from right.

OPPOSITE: *Bill, in a 1919 photo he labeled in his beautiful handwriting, showing him with the U.S. Army of Occupation.*

U.S. Army of Occupation
4th Infantry Division
Vallendar, Germany May 1919

Bill had been away for two years. It was time to go home. In late 1919, following his return to America, Bill Shemin was awarded impressive war medals for his heroism. He received the Silver Star, which was later replaced and upgraded to the Distinguished Service Cross, and the Purple Heart (for being wounded). Some of Bill's platoon

Bill's Distinguished Service Cross

Bill's Purple Heart Medal

members wanted him considered for a Medal of Honor for his heroic actions at the time, but he was passed over. He did not complain. He said that he was happy to be alive and to have served his country.

But there is more to this part of his story. Why had Bill not received a Medal of Honor like other brave soldiers of his time who performed heroic acts on the battlefield? Was this due to various levels of anti-Jewish feelings and policies of the times? It turns out Bill Shemin had been nominated for the medal but then denied it, with little explanation. Why?

It would be many more years before someone close to Bill would get an answer to that important question.

Back Home

Once he was home, Bill was ready to get back to work. Because he had been injured in Bazoches, Bill was granted a full scholarship to college. He enrolled at Syracuse University (SU), which was like a homecoming, since his original training as a forest ranger had been at a school affiliated with Syracuse. At SU, Bill reconnected with his love of forestry and passion for nature. He entered the Syracuse College of Forestry, where he enjoyed the outdoors and activities such as sawing logs.

Fun Fact: Bill Won Sawing Contest

When he was not in the classroom or on the football field, Bill found other activities to continue to challenge himself. One time he and another student won a contest for sawing through a huge, 14-inch log in just 30 seconds. A local newspaper that covered the event wrote at the time,

> "There's an echo of the world war in the feat of the duo who did the job in half a minute. Shemin was a sergeant of infantry in the big conflict. Sergeants were very busy men anyway and had to do things rapidly."

Legend has it that Bill's time still stands as a College of Forestry record.

Champions in Wood Sawing Contest
Arthur A. Davis and William Shemin

[S]TUDENTS OF FORESTRY ESTABLISH NEW RECORD

[Ar]thur A. Davis and William Shemin, [H]ill Sophomores, Saw Through 14-Inch Log in Exactly 30 Seconds.

[. . .] answer to the old query [. . .] much wood would a wood-[chuck] if a woodchuck could [wood]" It isn't even the boast-[cital] of greatness of accomplish-[ment] but it is presented as a logical [. . .] a championship at strenuous [. . .]ted in behalf of the New [Col]. . . Forestry at Syracuse [. . .] and particularly two sopho-[students therein.]

[. . .]y be records elsewhere, in [. . .] camps of Michigan or the [. . .] that equal it, but if so they [. . .]ated to this neck of the [. . .] until they do come, properly [. . .]ted the subjoined achieve-[ment . . .] accepted as a feat that [. . .] a championship [. . .] same moment the [were winning] world's honors at [. . .]

[. . . wo]uld it take you, reader, [. . . friend] to saw through [. . . log]? Four or five minutes [. . . wouldn't] it, perhaps more?

Well, Arthur A. Davis of New Hampshire and William Shemin of Brooklyn, aforementioned sophomores in the College of Forestry, turned the trick in exactly 30 seconds. The feat was performed at the annual barbecue of 300 students and 25 members of the faculty at Green lake, near Jamesville.

Corby and Pratt, sturdy and experienced seniors, took 31.2 seconds for the feat. Wetherby and Shane, strong and promising but still freshmen, consumed 49 seconds, while fourth honors went to Woolschlager and French, second senior team.

There's an echo of the world war in the feat of the duo who did the job in half a minute. Shemin was a sergeant of infantry in the big conflict. Sergeants were very busy men anyway and they had to do things rapidly. Shemin did so well for Uncle Sam in France that he was rewarded with the D. S. C. and he is a vocational board man at the local college, setting new records for himself and his alma mater.

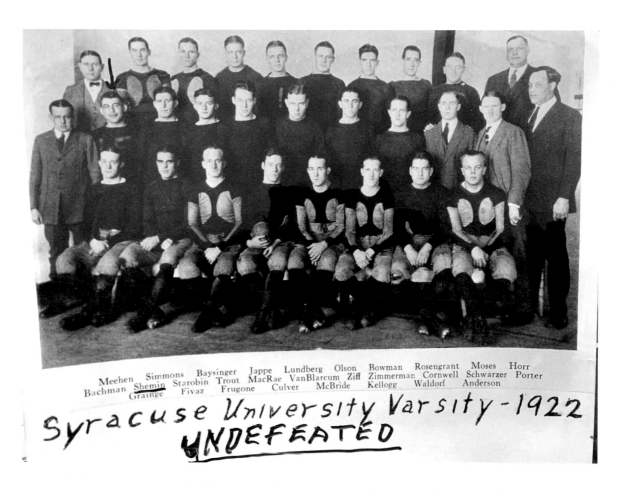

Meehen Simmons Baysinger Jappe Lundberg Olson Bowman Rosengrant Moses Horr
Bachman Shemin Starobin Trout MacRae VanBlarcum Ziff Zimmerman Cornwell Schwarzer Porter
Grainge Fivaz Frugone Culver McBride Kellogg Waldorf Anderson

Syracuse University Varsity - 1922
UNDEFEATED

Bill played varsity football in the fall and lacrosse in
the spring on the Syracuse teams today known as the
"Orange." Even though he had a concussion from his head
wound, and other war wounds acted up from time to time,
Bill still managed to perform as a top athlete.

Bill's degree from the Syracuse College of Forestry in 1923 inspired him to open his own nursery and greenhouse. He found the perfect location on Boston Post Road in the Bronx, New York. The start-up business was called Ivy Floral and Landscape Co. To honor his time in the army, Bill created a logo for his business that resembled leaves of ivy, like the ones on his 4th Infantry Division **insignia**.

Bill could usually be found with an axe or a hoe, enjoying his hard work and a life on the land, surrounded by his many plants. He loved his corner of the Bronx, where his business of trees, plants, flowers, and landscaping did well. His maple trees were planted through-

The 4th Infantry Division Ivy Insignia

The 4th Infantry Division's official nickname, "Ivy," is a play on words of the Roman Numeral IV or 4. Ivy leaves symbolize tenacity and fidelity, which are the basis of the division's motto: "Steadfast and Loyal." The second nickname, "Iron Horse," has been adopted to underscore the speed and power of the division and its soldiers. Bill Shemin would use the Ivy name and insignia from his 4th Division days in the name and logo for his landscaping business in civilian life.

out the five boroughs of New York City. No matter what Bill Shemin did, he found a way to make things work!

Right after he returned from war, Bill met and married his blue-eyed, red-haired sweetheart from Bayonne, Bertha Schiffer. Bertha was a kindergarten teacher and an accomplished pianist. They had three beautiful children, Elsie, Emanuel (Manny), and Ina Shemin.

At home, Bill was a devoted husband and father. He expected his children to do their best and depended upon them to work in the nursery. Everyone had to do their

Telephone: Fairbanks 4-3341

The Ivy Floral & Landscape Co.
WM. SHEMIN, Prop.

Florists and Landscape Contractors

Greenhouses and Nurseries

4000 BOSTON ROAD
Bronx N. Y. City

Near Dyre Ave. Station
on N. Y. B. W. R. R.

Bill Shemin June 1924
Boston Rd. Bronx N.Y. City

TOP: *Bill in the greenhouse, 1924.*

ABOVE: *Bill's business as it stood in the 1950s.*

share of the work to keep the business going. He taught his
children at an early age the value of hard work and the
value of a close family. And he was ahead of his time in
two important respects: He treated his son and daughters
equally and expected the same amount of physical work

from all of his children. Everyone had to lift the same heavy bags of soil! And all three children would go to college when many others in their age group at that time went straight to work upon graduation from high school.

Left to right: Ina, Emanuel, Elsie.

Bill was rough and tough, but he had been a hero on the fields of France, and now he was a hero to his family in the Bronx and beyond.

As the years passed, and Bill's business grew, he suffered more physical symptoms from his war injuries.

Bill had a hard time sleeping due to the pain from the shrapnel that was still lodged in his back. The pain and suffering of World War I never left him.

Left to right: Elsie, Manny, and Ina.

His children, Elsie, Ina, and Manny, learned to never, ever let a screen door slam at home because Bill would startle at a sudden loud noise. Their father's hearing was greatly damaged from the bullet that had lodged near his ear. Loud noises like a slamming door sounded too much like the explosions in no-man's-land.

Bill's sleep was haunted with troubling memories of his time in the war. His eldest daughter Elsie guessed that Bill probably suffered from what we now call PTSD, or **post-traumatic stress disorder**. "You could press on his back and feel the metal he lived with," she said. "There was a lot of it."

The impressions of her father and all that he had endured in World War I shaped Elsie's sense of purpose. She was inspired by his sense of duty and determination.

As Bill Shemin grew older, he took great pleasure in gathering the family around him at his summer home in Chazy on Lake Champlain. He would put his children to work as if he were still a sergeant in the army. Here, Bill maintained his lifetime love of plants and gardening, raising a couple of acres of fruits, vegetables, and flowers. And this was the place where the future generations of Shemins were taught how to garden and the sacred nature of flying, saluting, and folding the American flag.

Anti-Semitism in World War I

William Shemin never lost the hard edge that came from being a sergeant in World War I, but Elsie rarely heard her father tell long war stories unless she asked him to share.

In so many ways, being raised by Bill Shemin was like being in basic training in the army. Bill liked to order people around all the time, even his own children! But when Elsie was just twelve, her father's strict behavior and his unflagging commitment to his country began to make more sense. He wasn't mean. He was a man of duty and honor. Bill completed his military duties because it was the right thing to do. Getting a medal was not something Bill needed or wanted. He served his country because it was important to do so. He would say, "War is not about medals, it's about achieving goals and saving lives."

Elsie recalled a time when Bill's good friend Jim Pritchard, whom Bill had rescued in Bazoches, came to visit. Jim said, "Your father never got the medal he deserved because he was a Jew." Those words stuck with Elsie. She needed to fix that. Her father deserved better.

NATHAN MERENBACH
ATTORNEY AT LAW
1234 NORIEGA STREET
SAN FRANCISCO, CALIFORNIA 94122
PHONE (415) 681-3113

July 2, 1974

Dear Mrs. Roth:

Ever since I obtained your address from Leo Jereb, the Editor of the Ivy Leaves (January, 1974), I intended to write a brief note to you.

I am enclosing a photostat of my letter to the Editor. One thing the letter did not contain, which I wish to add. Your father and I, as far as I remember, were the only Jews in our company, and this, perhaps, added to our feeling of mutual closeness.

I indeed grieve his passing, but, unfortunately, all of us veterans of World War I are living on borrowed time.

Most sincerely,

Nathan Merenbach

Nathan Merenbach.

P.S. - A similar note was addressed by me to your brother Emanuel Shemin.

Letter to Elsie from Nathan Merenbach, one of Bill's company members, remembering how he and Bill were the only two Jewish men in the company.

Some Background on Anti-Semitism in the Army at the Time of World War I

American Jews like William Shemin had been eager to fight for their country in World War I. Many of them had the same motivation as Bill—to show that they were "real Americans" and "real patriots," just like everyone else, and to respond to the call of duty from the country that had welcomed their families. Jews represented around 3 percent of the U.S. population when the war started, yet they were "over-represented" among the soldiers in the Great War, making up 6 percent of the members of the army in World War I.

This was a time in American history when discrimination toward Jews was a little more hidden than it was towards African Americans. Top colleges, for example, allowed bright Jewish students in, but had a secret quota system to prevent "too many" Jews from enrolling. Those same colleges might not allow an African American student admission at all. In a similar way, few Medals of Honor were awarded to Jewish battlefield heroes in World War I. William Shemin was only the fourth Medal of Honor recipient in World War I among approximately 250,000 Jewish soldiers. And some military units were overseen by generals or commanders who were openly anti-Semitic and would never approve a Medal of Honor recommendation for a Jewish soldier.

*African Americans fought bravely for the United States
but were not well treated upon their return home.*

World War I had been a clash of countries with different races and religions, so it was perhaps no surprise there was a rise in **anti-Semitic** feelings and **racism** in the United States during the war. Many soldiers in World War I were challenged by ongoing **discrimination**. To say so plainly that Bill Shemin did not receive the Medal of Honor because some people didn't like his Jewish faith upset Elsie greatly.

Family Man

Bravery was Bill Shemin's gift. His children, grandchildren, great-grandchildren, and the extended Shemin family are his legacy.

Bill's heroism came from his strong moral character and the values Bill placed on family, faith, and hard work.

TOP: *Bill and his wife Bertha with their grandchildren in the 1950s.*
ABOVE LEFT: *Bertha in the 1950s.* ABOVE RIGHT: *Bill in the 1950s.*

Bill did not forget his army friends and they did not forget him. He helped many veterans find jobs and receive medical help. He attended Legion of Valor and veterans meetings and conventions, and was especially involved with the Jewish War Veterans. He headed the New York chapter of the Legion of Valor. Despite his many injuries, his personal sacrifices, and all the death and destruction he had seen, Bill talked about the U.S. Army with the reverence of a true patriot. When the winds of World War II started to blow and the anti-American, pro-Hitler **German American Bund** started rallying in the Bronx,

Bill Shemin on his way to a meeting he had organized in the late 1930s between the Jewish War Veterans and the German American Bund to demand they stop their anti-Jewish and racial verbal attacks.

68

Bill stood them down and demanded they stop their anti-American activities. After Pearl Harbor and the U.S. entry into World War II in the 1940s, Bill actually tried to volunteer, despite his age and wounds from the last world war.

At the time of his death in 1973, Bill's fourteen grandkids were thankful, too, for the influence that Bill had on their upbringing. He shared his love of America and boundless patriotism with them throughout their lives. As President Barack Obama said during the Medal of Honor ceremony, "Bill taught them how to salute. He taught them the correct way to raise the flag every morning and lower and fold it every night. He taught them how to be Americans."

1968   Grandfather ~ **Montfaucon** ~ Granddaughter   2018

On the left, Bill at the Montfaucon memorial for the 50th anniversary of the Meuse-Argonne Offensive in 1968. On the right, one of Bill's granddaughters, Suzanne Shemin Katz, visits the same site for the 100th anniversary in 2018.

Bill and Bertha's 40th Wedding Anniversary photo, June 1968.

The Letter

When Bill's granddaughter Sara Cass had her **bat mitzvah** in 1967, he sent a letter which, even in his elder years, displayed his elegant handwriting. The letter contains the simple and true secrets to Bill Shemin's success in life. He followed these rules in sports, at school, in the army, and in his family life:

1. Stay with your religion.
2. Keep up strong ties with your family and don't drift away from them as you get older.
3. Don't be afraid of hard work and try to give a little more than what you are required to do.

William Shemin, D. S. C.
West Chazy, New York   May 2nd 1967

Dear Sarabeth:

We are getting ready to leave Hot Springs and after a few days stop over with Elsie in Missouri, we will be home to help you celebrate your thirtheenth Birthday.

This will be an important event for you, and the people there will be saying nice things to you. "Sarabeth" we would like to leave with you a few words, that we would like you to remember, as you go through life.

The first is, always stay with your religion. Second, keep up strong ties with your family, dont drift away from them, as you get older. Last, dont be afraid of hard work, and try to give a little more than what you are required to do. If you do all of these things your parents will be proud of you.

Enclosed is a gift for your birthday. We will see you soon and send our love, and congratulations.

Grand Ma and Grand Pa Shemin

71

Sgt. William Shemin, 4th Division, 47th Infantry, Company G, received this Victory Medal in 1919. The five clasps represent major campaigns in which he fought. In 1919, he was recommended for the Citation in Orders, which later became the Silver Star award, for action in the Aisne-Marne, Vesle Bazoches campaign, which occurred August 7–10, 1918. After further review, Shemin was instead awarded the Distinguished Service Cross, a higher decoration along with a wound chevron, which later became the Purple Heart medal. On June 2, 2015, almost 100 years after the action, President Barack Obama upgraded the Distinguished Service Cross to the Medal of Honor.

Sgt. Shemin was awarded the Defensive Sector clasp for action in both the Vesle and Toulon sectors. It is extremely rare to be awarded five of six possible clasps; it signifies a tremendous amount of time at the front and under fire.

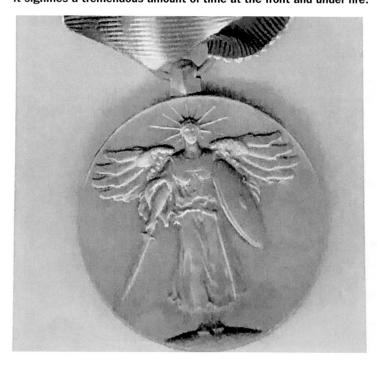

Elsie Shemin-Roth: A Daughter on a Mission

For many years after her father's death, Elsie had been thinking about finding a way to get proper recognition for her father's heroism. The road to awarding Bill Shemin the Medal of Honor would take almost fifteen years of research, finding the right connections, telling the facts, and a devotion to the strong work ethic that she inherited from her father. Relentless and **tenacious**, Elsie Shemin-Roth would stop at nothing until that medal was awarded to Sergeant William Shemin.

In 2002, Elsie noticed an article about legislation passed in Congress that would allow those who had received medals for bravery in World War II, the Korean War, and Vietnam, to be reconsidered **posthumously** for the Medal of Honor if their family and friends could show they had been denied consideration for the Medal of Honor because of their religion or race.

This gave Elsie the spark of an idea. If the cases of soldiers from World War II and Korea could be reopened, why not World War I? Elsie felt that World War I vets should also have a shot for a Medal of Honor review. "Although my father always told me his war experience was *never* about medals," Elsie said, "I knew in my heart he was deserving of the highest military award for valor—the Medal of Honor."

Who Is Elsie Shemin-Roth?

Elsie's bravery and determination did not start with her crusade to honor her father and other World War I soldiers whose acts of heroism had been overlooked because of racial or religious discrimination against them. She had been breaking boundaries and fighting for what is right for a long time. Bill Shemin was a hero on the battlefield and Elsie is a hero in her own way as well.

A registered nurse, Elsie helped people all over the world. Her missions started in Ethiopia in the 1980s. Elsie aided the Jews there to escape from danger and assessed their needs to prepare for evacuation to Israel. During the war in Bosnia, Elsie brought $10 million dollars' worth of pharmaceutical, medical, and clothing supplies through Hadassah, traveling there three times to help Muslims, Serbs, and Croats. She was assisted there by a small Jewish community that chose to remain throughout the war in Bosnia. Elsie also spent the whole Gulf War in Tel Aviv, under Scud missile fire, working as a nurse with high-risk seniors in Ichilov Hospital. In addition, her social action work included a lifetime of leadership in the Jewish community and other important causes in St Louis, Missouri.

Elsie found a treasure **trove** of recommendation letters, witness lists, and other documents to verify how her father risked his life during battle.

There was just one problem: Elsie had to get a new law passed before her father could even be considered for the Medal of Honor. In 2011, the William Shemin Jewish World War I Veterans Act was passed. This was no small feat. At the time, the U.S. Congress was bitterly divided between Democrats and Republicans who could not agree on anything. But Elsie, with the help of a few dedicated members of the House and Senate, brought both sides together to pass the bill.

Now Elsie was one step closer to having her father receive the recognition he deserved—the Medal of Honor. Fortunately, Bill Shemin carefully saved a document that had the names and identification numbers of six soldiers that witnessed the action. It was a military requirement that only an officer's account of the action would be acceptable as a witness. Bill had three officer accounts with the backup of three enlisted men. Even with this hundred-year-old document, there was still a long way to go. Three review boards were waiting to do their work. They were the Secretary of the Army, the Secretary of Defense, and finally the President of the United States of America. But just like her father, Elsie had already made the seemingly impossible start to be possible.

Company "G" 47th Infantry,
American E.F.   Germany.
20   May   1919.

From: Commanding Officer Company "G" 47th Infantry.

To: Commanding General 4th Division.
              (Thru Military Channels)

Subject: Recommendation for D.S.C.

1. It is recommended that Sgt. William Shemin be awarded a distinguished service cross for conduct specified below:

(a) Sergeant William Shemin(556173),Company "G" 47th Infantry.

(b) August 7,8 and 9, 1918. Place: Near Bazoches,Vesle River France

(c) Next of Kin: Father - Mary Shemin, 71 West 52nd St. Bayonne N.J.

(d) Sgt. William Shemin showed extraordinary heroism above and beyond the call of duty near Bazoches,Vesle River France jon Aug 7,8 and 9th 1918; Sgt Shemin repeatedly and at the most imminent risk of life and limb exposed himself to the fire of the enemy to bring in from the open fields before our position, which was constantly swept by heavy fire, several wounded comrades. Sgt. Shemin, at the beginning of the action a junior non-commisioned officer in his platoon was required by casualties to take command. He distinguished himself by exhibiting the most efficient qualities of leadership. Cool,calm, intelligent and personally utterly fearless, he was a big factor in maintaining splendid morale and tactical efficiency of his platoon.

(e) Witnesses: Major Robert T. Clark,47th Infantry
                Capt. R.L. Purdon, 47th Infantry
                1st Lieu't Henry C. Martin, 47th Infantry
                Sgt. Louis Sides, Company "G" 47th Infantry.
                Sgt. Lyle Nolan, Company "G" 47th Infantry.
                Sgt. Joseph Balash, Company "G" 47th Infantry.

There are no witnesses from other branches of the service.

Frank Lee

(Frank Lee)
1st Lt. 47th Inf.
Comd'g Company.

Without this "witness document" (the 1919 letter), Sgt. Shemin would not have been awarded the Distinguished Service Cross, the upgrade to the Medal of Honor would not have happened, and this book could not have been written.

Amendment to H.R. 1540 - National Defense Authorization Act for Fiscal Year 2012

William Shemin Jewish World War I Veterans Act

May 26, 2011

Mr./Madam Speaker, I am proud to rise in support of an amendment that would allow for the review of service records of eligible Jewish American veterans from World War I. I want to thank Chairman McKeon and Ranking Member Smith, along with my colleagues who cosponsored the legislation for their support of this important issue.

We owe much to the patriotic Americans who have worn and are wearing the uniforms of our nation's Armed Forces. Our country has been blessed to have citizens who have selflessly volunteered to defend our natio and freedom.

Unfortunately, qualified soldiers have not been considered for the Medal of Honor, the highest military decoration awarded by our government, due to discrimination. In 2001, Congress passed the Leonard Kravitz Jewish War Veterans Act, which had broad bipartisan support. This important piece of legislation presented Jewish soldiers the opportunity to receive the Medal of Honor for their service in World War II. However, Jewish veterans of World War I faced similar discrimination and yet, have not been afforded the opportunity to receive recognition for their service. Last Congress, this amendment was included as part of an en bloc group of amendments that was agreed to by the House by a 416-to-1 vote in the National Defense Authorization Act, H.R. 5136.

William Shemin was a Jewish American who earned the Distinguished Service Cross (DSC) in 1918 for saving three of his fellow soldiers' lives during an intense three-day battle in France, while also leading his platoon in combat after more senior soldiers were wounded or killed. Shemin passed away in 1973, but his daughter, Elsie Shemin-Roth, a resident of my district, has passionately worked on behalf of her father's military legacy.

This amendment builds upon past legislation to recognize the sacrifices of Jewish soldiers during World War I.

I urge my colleagues to join me in supporting an amendment that honors the work of these brave veterans.

Thank you, Mr./Madam Speaker. I reserve the balance of my time.

Blaine Luetkemeyer
Member of Congress

Missouri Congressman Blaine Luetkemeyer's letter of support for the amendment to review the service records of eligible Jewish American veterans from World War I who were discriminated against and should have been considered for the Medal of Honor.

SGT William Shemin, USA
2 June 2015

The Medal of Honor

After fifteen years, so much effort, and hearing "sorry, no," to many requests, Elsie finally heard the news she wanted to hear. President Obama approved the Medal of Honor request in 2015. The same William Shemin Act was also used to reconsider the heroism of other World War I soldiers who had been overlooked for the Medal of Honor because of discrimination, and that included the African American hero, Henry Johnson. A White House ceremony was convened for June 2, 2015, to present the Medal of Honor posthumously to William Shemin and Henry Johnson. On that occasion, President Barack Obama said:

> It has taken a long time for Henry Johnson and William Shemin to receive the recognition they deserve. And there are surely others whose heroism is still unacknowledged and uncelebrated. We have work to do, as a nation, to make sure that all our heroes' stories are told. And we'll keep at it, no matter how long it takes. America is the country we are today because of people like Henry and William— Americans who signed up to serve and rose to meet their responsibilities—and then went beyond. The least we can do is to say: We know who you are. We know what you did for us. We are forever grateful.

OPPOSITE: *The Medal of Honor posthumously awarded to Sergeant William Shemin.*

At a press conference, Elsie announced to the country with pride, "My father's story can be told in eleven simple words: 'Discrimination hurts. A wrong has been made right. All is forgiven.'"

President Obama further said:

Elsie, as much as America meant to your father, he means even more to America. It takes our nation too long sometimes to say so—because Sergeant Shemin served at a time when the contributions and heroism of Jewish Americans in uniform were too often overlooked. But William Shemin saved American lives. He stood for our nation with honor. And so, it is my privilege, on behalf of the American people, to make this right and finally award the Medal of Honor to Sergeant William Shemin.

MEDAL OF HONOR CITATION
FOR WILLIAM SHEMIN

The President of the United States of America, authorized by Act of Congress, March 3, 1863, has awarded in the name of Congress the Medal of Honor to Sergeant William Shemin, United States Army.

Sergeant William Shemin distinguished himself by extraordinary acts of heroism at the risk of his life above and beyond the call of duty while serving as a shooter with G Company, 2nd Battalion, 47th Infantry Regiment, 4th Division, American Expeditionary Forces, in connection with combat operations against an armed enemy on the Vesle River, near Bazoches, France from August 7th to August 9th, 1918.

Sergeant Shemin upon three different occasions left cover and crossed an open space of 150 yards, repeatedly exposing himself to heavy machine gun and rifle fire to rescue wounded. After officers and senior noncommissioned officers had become casualties, Sergeant Shemin took command of the platoon and displayed great initiative under fire until wounded on August 9th. Sergeant Shemin's extraordinary heroism and selflessness above and beyond the call of duty are in keeping with the highest traditions of the military service and reflect great credit upon himself with G Company, 2nd Battalion, 47th Infantry Regiment, 4th Division, American Expeditionary Forces, and the United States Army.

Sixty Shemin family members attended the White House ceremony as part of the historic thank you ceremony that had been delayed for almost one hundred years! The family included Bill's two daughters (Elsie and Ina), thirteen grandchildren, many more great-grandchildren, and numerous cousins and their families. Obama joked that there was a whole "platoon of Shemins" in the room.

Three generations of the Shemin family (and Syracuse University graduates) celebrate the fourth generation and William Shemin's Medal of Honor presentation at the White House on June 2, 2015. Front row (L–R): Ina Shemin Bass '53, holding the MOH, and Elsie Shemin-Roth '51 (daughters of William Shemin). Back row (L–R): Scott Bass '15 (great-grandson), William Cass '08 (great-grandson), Rachel Forman '05 (great-granddaughter), Seth Forman (Rachel's husband) '04, Leslie Shemin-Lester '84 (granddaughter), and Sam Cass '13 (great-grandson).

Elsie and her sister Ina accepted Bill's medal on behalf of forgotten soldiers, too. "The supreme honor is in the name of William Shemin, but it would please him if it were also dedicated to the fallen, the survivors, and their families." At the White House ceremony, President Obama linked William Shemin and Henry Johnson together in American history with these words:

> America honors two of her sons who served in World War I, nearly a century ago. These two soldiers were roughly the same age, dropped into the battlefields of France at roughly the same time. They both risked their own lives to save the lives of others. They both left us decades ago, before we could give them the full recognition that they deserved. But it's never too late to say thank you. Today, we present America's highest military decoration, the Medal of Honor, to Private Henry Johnson and Sergeant William Shemin.

Recognizing that Henry Johnson had no living family members to accept the medal on his behalf (although he was well-represented at the White House ceremony by supporters of his old 369th unit, often referred to as the Harlem Hellfighters), Elsie Shemin instructed future generations of Shemins to use every opportunity to tell William Shemin's story as well as Henry Johnson's story and to make the fight against anti-Semitism into a wider fight against discrimination of all types.

Staff Sergeant Jonell Gittens lays a wreath at the grave of a fallen member of the Harlem Hellfighters in a World War I cemetery in France.

Sgt. Gittens, a member of the 369th Sustainment Brigade, the modern incarnation of Henry Johnson's old unit, joined the Shemin family for a 2018 hundredth anniversary "In the Footsteps" tour of the Medal of Honor battlefields in France for the two heroes, William Shemin and Henry Johnson.

An Inspiration

In addition to the medals and tributes, plaques of William Shemin were created at the Ranger School and at Syracuse University. He received entry into the Hall of Heroes in the Pentagon. And then, he received a very special tribute. It was fitting for a man who cared deeply for his neighbors.

In Bayonne, New Jersey, where Bill had been raised as a young boy, the City Council decided to name a school after him.

Elsie said, "A ceremony naming a school after my father in his hometown means as much to me as when the President gave us the Medal of Honor . . . My father taught us to always give back more than you're asked to do. He had a wonderful generosity and sense of honor. If this country needs you, you go."

Bayonne Schools Superintendent John Niesz said, "We are renaming a school for a hometown hero who went above and beyond. By dedicating this school, students will think about those who served and may well follow in his example to do what is right."

Councilman-at-Large Juan Perez, who initially suggested the renaming of the school, said, "Sgt. Shemin was an outstanding soldier. He was a young man who

---

Bayonne: City of Medal of Honor Recipients

Bill Shemin was not the first Medal of Honor recipient to be recognized by his hometown of Bayonne. This New Jersey city of 65,000 people also claims two other Medal of Honor recipients in its past. Before renaming its largest elementary school, with its diverse student body of 1,200 students in grades Pre-K through 8, after Sgt. Shemin, Bayonne had named the county park in honor of Stephen R. Gregg—a World War II Medal of Honor recipient—and named former Public School No. 14 after Nicholas Oresko, who also was a World War II Medal of Honor recipient.

was raised in Bayonne (and) went into the Army and distinguished himself."

When the Midtown Community School was renamed the William Shemin Midtown Community School, there was a day of celebration. Students, teachers, and staff put together a show to honor Sgt. Shemin. Elsie and other members of the Shemin and Pritchard families attended.

A local Bayonne official called the celebration "a special day in a special city for a special man."

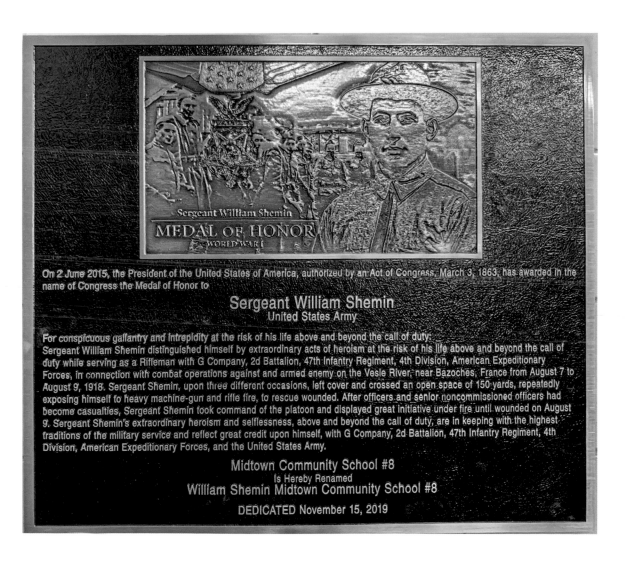

Sergeant William Shemin
MEDAL OF HONOR
WORLD WAR I

On 2 June 2015, the President of the United States of America, authorized by an Act of Congress, March 3, 1863, has awarded in the name of Congress the Medal of Honor to

Sergeant William Shemin
United States Army

For conspicuous gallantry and intrepidity at the risk of his life above and beyond the call of duty: Sergeant William Shemin distinguished himself by extraordinary acts of heroism at the risk of his life above and beyond the call of duty while serving as a Rifleman with G Company, 2d Battalion, 47th Infantry Regiment, 4th Division, American Expeditionary Forces, in connection with combat operations against and armed enemy on the Vesle River, near Bazoches, France from August 7 to August 9, 1918. Sergeant Shemin, upon three different occasions, left cover and crossed an open space of 150 yards, repeatedly exposing himself to heavy machine-gun and rifle fire, to rescue wounded. After officers and senior noncommissioned officers had become casualties, Sergeant Shemin took command of the platoon and displayed great initiative under fire until wounded on August 9. Sergeant Shemin's extraordinary heroism and selflessness, above and beyond the call of duty, are in keeping with the highest traditions of the military service and reflect great credit upon himself, with G Company, 2d Battalion, 47th Infantry Regiment, 4th Division, American Expeditionary Forces, and the United States Army.

Midtown Community School #8
Is Hereby Renamed
William Shemin Midtown Community School #8

DEDICATED November 15, 2019

OPPOSITE: *Images from the ceremony in 2019, renaming the school to William Shemin Community School.*

RIGHT: *Principal Dr. Wachera Ragland-Brown at the ceremony in 2019.*

BELOW: *Elsie and Ina (center) with the Pritchard Family.*

89

Making a Difference

In 2016, a monument was erected at the cemetery where Bill Shemin was buried. In the Baron Hirsch Cemetery on Staten Island, New York, people gathered.

The Shemin family planted two trees to honor Bill Shemin and Henry Johnson, the two brave soldiers who were finally honored with the medal they both deserved.

On a blazing hot day, the family gathered there for its first viewing, joined by groups of Jewish War Veterans, supporters of the Harlem Hellfighters, high school ROTC members, Vietnam War Veterans, and diverse friends and community members from Bayonne, Staten Island, and many other places. The crowd spanned at least four generations, including children and teens. The camaraderie was heartfelt as everyone reflected on the examples set by Bill Shemin and Henry Johnson. The only thing that would have made the moment more perfect would had have been if Bill and Henry were there, standing tall alongside their families and their admirers.

A hero can change the world and the people in it. William Shemin did it. You can, too.

OPPOSITE: *Even the youngest members of the extended Shemin family participated in the events at the Baron Hirsch Cemetery.*

Tributes were made for both William and Henry with **(TOP PHOTO)** *Command Sergeant Major Louis Wilson from the New York Army National Guard representing Henry Johnson and* **(BOTTOM PHOTO)** *Dan Burstein representing William Shemin and the Shemin Family.*

ROTC cadets, veterans, and other members of the military community paying tribute to William and Henry at the Baron Hirsch Cemetery.
NEXT PAGE: *Plaque at Baron Hirsch Cemetery honoring both William and Henry installed by the Shemin family in 2016.*

In Honor of Two United States Army World War One Medal of Honor Heroes
These Japanese Maple Trees were planted

Sgt. William Shemin

Final Resting Place
Baron Hirsch Cemetery

Sgt. Henry Johnson

Final Resting Place
Arlington National Cemetery

ALMOST 100 YEARS AFTER "THE GREAT WAR"
EACH RECIEVED THE MEDAL OF HONOR FROM
PRESIDENT BARACK OBAMA
AT THE WHITE HOUSE ON JUNE 2, 2015

THE DELAY IN THEIR BEING HONORED WAS DUE TO
RELIGIOUS DISCRIMINATION FOR SGT. SHEMIN WHO WAS JEWISH AND
RACIAL DISCRIMINATION FOR SGT. JOHNSON WHO WAS AFRICAN AMERICAN.

HAVING NO FAMILY, THE SHEMIN FAMILY HAVE PROUDLY EMBRACED
SGT. JOHNSON INTO THEIR FAMILY'S LEGACY.

MAY THEIR STORY OF BRAVERY BE A BLESSING AND INSPIRATION
TO BE REMEMBERED BY ALL
FROM GENERATION TO GENERATION.
L'DOR V'DOR

"Change will not come if we wait for
some other person or some other time.
We are the ones we've been waiting for.
We are the change that we seek."

—PRESIDENT BARACK OBAMA

Postscript
The Fight Against
Discrimination of All Kinds
Continues . . .

Since Elsie's pioneering victory in 2015, we have seen both progress and setbacks in America. On the one hand, there is a rising wave of hate crimes and attacks against African Americans, Asians, Latinos, Native American, Jews, women, and other minority groups. On the other hand, the military has continued to work to right some of the wrongs of the past following the landmark award of Medals of Honor to William and Henry seven years ago. Today there is an active campaign in the U.S. Congress to award a Medal of Honor to Marcelino Serna, a heroic World War I era soldier from Texas, who was denied consideration for the Medal of Honor in his lifetime because he was born in Mexico. Other minority soldiers from World War II and Vietnam have had their cases reconsidered for Medals of Honor in light of new review processes that take discrimination during those eras into account. And a commission on renaming American military bases has recommended that a Louisiana facility currently named for a Confederate general be renamed for Henry Johnson. So, there continues to be progress, even as the warning signs of rising hatred and injustice in our society continue to flash red.

We hope this book inspires people to continue the fight for justice and equality for all people.

—**September, 2022**

Exhibit at the Weitzman National Museum of American Jewish History, Philadelphia, Pennsylvania, paying tribute to both Sergeant William Shemin, with artifacts from his life (on the left) and Henry Johnson (far right).

A display featuring Sgt. Shemin's World War I memorabilia at the American Jewish Historical Society's 2017 exhibit, "1917: How One Year Changed the World."

The challenge coin had its origin during ancient Rome. Coins were presented for outstanding accomplishments and exchanged during visits. They were meant to be a reward and to build morale. Challenge coins have been used in the U.S. military at least since WWI. They came into wider use in more recent American wars. Elsie designed the one for William Shemin (**MIDDLE PHOTO, WITH FRONT AND BACK OF COIN**) as well as the renderings (**TOP ROW**) of the Medals of Honor for William and Henry. Challenge coin (**BELOW, FRONT AND BACK**) made for the 369th Sustainment Brigade-Harlem Hellfighters, the modern unit that has inherited Henry Johnson's legacy.

STARS AND STRIPES
HEROES 2015

Glossary

alliances   Forces that join to help each other.

anti-Semitic   Being hostile or prejudiced against Jewish people.

armistice   Agreement to stop fighting a war for a period.

artillery   Large guns used in warfare on land.

barbed wire   Wire with spikes that is used to make fences during warfare to prevent movement.

barracks   Building or group of buildings used to house soldiers.

bat mitzvah   A religious ceremony for a Jewish girl when she reaches the age of thirteen that signifies she is ready to assume religious responsibilities and become a full member of the Jewish community and its rituals.

campaign   A series of military operations.

casualties   People killed or injured in a war or accident.

competitor   Someone who is opposing you and trying to win something that you also want.

continents   Any of the world's continuous expanses of land like Africa, Antarctica, Australia, Europe, North America, and South America.

deployed   Movement of troops into position for military action.

destination   The place where something is going or being sent.

discrimination   Unjust or unfair treatment of specific groups of people usually based on race, religion, gender, ethnicity, beliefs, skin color, etc.

dodge   A quick movement to avoid someone or something.

drafted   Selected to go somewhere for a certain purpose.

duty   A moral or legal responsibility.

OPPOSITE: *Henry Johnson and William Shemin on the front cover of* Stars and Stripes, *2015, with other Medal of Honor recipients representing different wars in which Americans fought.*

enlist   Enroll in the armed services.

ethnic   Relating to group of people within a population that shares certain common cultural history or traditions.

front lines   Part of an army that is closest to the enemy.

German American Bund   A German-American Nazi organization established in the United States in 1936 to promote a favorable view of Hitler's Germany.

honored   Seen with great respect.

immigrants   People who come to live permanently in a foreign country.

infantry   Soldiers marching or fighting on foot.

insignia   Emblem or badge that shows rank or membership.

landsman   A fellow countryman/woman.

military   Relating to the armed forces.

mustard gas   A dangerous liquid that produces a vapor or gas highly toxic to the body and used in chemical weapons.

neutral   Not choosing a side during a conflict.

newsies   People (typically boys) who sold newspapers in city streets in the early twentieth century.

no-man's-land   An unoccupied area between two opposing armies.

occupation   The holding and control of an area by a foreign military force.

outhouse   Outdoor toilet with no plumbing.

opportunity   Circumstance that makes it possible to do something.

patriotic   Devotion to and support of one's country.

penmanship   A person's handwriting.

perished   Died or disappeared and presumed dead.

platoon   A unit of the military made up of a small number of soldiers. A light infantry rifle platoon has 39 soldiers, for example.

pogrom   Organized massacre of specific ethnic group, especially Jews in Russia.

posthumously   After the person's death.

post-traumatic stress disorder   A condition of mental or emotional stress occurring as a result of injury or witnessing a terrifying event.

quarters   A place for people to live.

raids   Sudden attacks on an enemy.

racism   Prejudice and belief that one race is distinguished as inferior and another as superior.

recruit   To enlist someone as a member of a group for such things as sports or the military.

Regiment   Unit of the army.

sacrifice   To give up something for an ideal or belief.

segregated   Set apart from each other such as separated along racial lines.

sentry   A soldier stationed to keep guard.

shrapnel   Fragments of a bomb, shell, or other object thrown out by an explosion, killing or wounding a soldier or civilian. Named for its inventor, Henry Shrapnel (1761–1842), an English artillery officer.

skirmish   Minor fight in a war as part of a larger battle.

submarine   Warship that moves underwater, usually armed with missiles.

surrendered   Giving up to the enemy and submitting to their authority.

tenacious   Persistent in pursuing something of value, such as a goal.

trench   Narrow ditch dug by troops as shelter from enemy fire.

trench foot   This painful condition that damages feet after standing in cold water or mud for too long killed an estimated 2,000 Americans and 75,000 British soldiers during WWI.

trove   A valuable collection.

tsar   The title for the ruler of Russia before the 1917 revolution.

victorious   Triumphant after a win or victory.

Western Front   The 400-plus-mile stretch of land that was the main stage of war during World War I.

Yiddish   A language used by Jewish people in central and Eastern Europe that was originally a combination of German with words from Hebrew and bits of several modern languages.

Questions to Think About

1. Who is one hero you know and why would you call that person a hero?

2. What would motivate you to join the military during a war to defend your country?

3. What is one reason you would leave high school before graduation to do something very important?

4. Just as Sgt. Shemin was forced to risk his own life or save the life of fellow soldiers, what would you have done in the same situation?

5. What is one thing you have done in your life that required bravery?

6. What is one thing that you had to work hard for that you had to tell yourself to not give up in order to achieve?

OPPOSITE: *Bill Shemin and Theron "Ted" Dalrymple, his dear friend from their days at the Ranger School in upstate New York. Bill was from the big city and Ted was from the farm. Both served in the U.S. Armed Forces with distinction, both earning awards for bravery in action. Bill was wounded several times; sadly, Ted was killed in action.*

Ina Bass and Elsie Shemin-Roth represent their father while Command Sergeant Major Louis Wilson, New York Army National Guard, represents William Henry Johnson as Shemin and Johnson are inducted into the Hall of Heroes at the Pentagon, June 3, 2015.

Acknowledgments

It takes a village to raise a child and it took a village to bring the idea for this children's book to reality.

We wish to express our deepest appreciation to the many members of our literary and professional team: Eve Feldman, children's book author, who made our first step possible and developed the foundational outline; Laura Dower, the developmental editor who helped us to add drama, color, and detail to the book; David Wilk, our publisher, who supported this project from the start and oversaw all aspects of the book's production with expertise and sage counsel; Beth Tondreau, our designer responsible for the beautiful look of the book that allowed the William Shemin story to be told in such a vivid manner; Gary Bullock, illustrator extraordinaire who understood and helped to tell the William Shemin story with his realistic, dramatic, and engaging illustrations; Julie O'Connor, photographer, who provided artistic insight into the selection and organization of the photos, improved their quality, and advised on the telling of the story at many points.

Special thanks to the William Shemin Midtown Community School in Bayonne, New Jersey, and in particular to Dr. Wachera Wrangland-Brown, Principal, Patricia Dziubek, Assistant Principal, James Pondillo, Assistant Principal, and Tonya Elisha Mele, teacher, all of whom provided valuable input and suggestions. We also appreciate the support of the Bayonne Board of Education, and Superintendent John Niesz.

Thank you to the Weitzman National Museum of American Jewish History in Philadelphia for assistance with photos and its general support of the William Shemin legacy.

Many family members were actively involved in helping this project come to life: Elsie Shemin-Roth, Ina Shemin Bass, Carolyn Roth, William Roth, Eddie Roth, Elisa Roth, David Burstein, Alan Blumberg, William Cass, and Sam Cass. A special thank you to Ken and Caitlin Shemin, Randy Shemin, and Richard and Susan Shemin. Other family members who provided support include Rhoda Shemin, Suzanne and Stuart Katz (including Stu's help with photos and photography), Grace and Louis Goldstein, Leslie and Andy Lester, Julie Bass Divens, Jonathan Goldstein, Evelyn Trichon, and Dan Forman.

Thanks as well to F. Robert Stein, Adam Guha, Jeremy Townsend, Diane Kraut, Camille Cline, Kemper Bernstein, and Max Weisner.

A special thank you to friends, especially Arne de Keijzer and Laura Kutnick, who reviewed the text and offered valuable suggestions.

Special thanks to Jim Pritchard Jr. (son of Bill Shemin's good friend Jim Pritchard) and his family for their support of this book.

Important figures in American public life have supported Elsie's efforts over the years and many of them lent us their wisdom for this book as well. The list is truly too long to mention everyone here, but we would be remiss if we did not take note of several of these great allies of the William Shemin legacy: President Barack Obama, Congressman Blaine Luetkemeyer, Senator Claire McCaskill, Senator Chuck Schumer, General Daniel Allyn (Ret., Vice Chief of Staff of the US Army), Major General David Hodne (Commanding General, 4th Infantry Division, Fort Carson, CO), Col. Erwin Burtnick

(Ret., Jewish War Veterans), Command Sergeant Major (Ret.) Louis Wilson, Col. Richard Goldenberg (US Army National Guard), Sergeant Major of the Army (Ret.) Daniel Dailey, Rabbi Jeffrey Stiffman (Rabbi Emeritus, Temple Shaare Emeth, St. Louis, MO), Councilman Juan Perez (Bayonne, NJ), Josh Perelman (Chief Curator, Weitzman National Museum of American Jewish History), Michael Cline (Museum Director, 4th Infantry Division Museum), Steve Ruhnke (Retired Curator, 4th Infantry Division Museum), Jonathan Casey (Archivist, WWI Museum), Patrick Osborn (Curator, National Archives), the Congregational Medal of Honor Society including Catherine Metcalf (Executive Director of Education), Victoria Kueck (Director of Operations,) and Laura Jowdy (Archivist), Mike Venso (Military and Firearms Curator, Missouri Historical Society, Soldier's Memorial Military Museum, St. Louis, MO), Robert Babcock (President of 4th Infantry Division Association), Dr. David S. Frey (Professor of History and Director, Center for Holocaust and Genocide Studies, West Point), Senior Supply Sergeant Jonell A. Gittens, and Jack Pirozzi (Executive Director, Major Gifts, Washington University).

More thank-yous: Brad R. Carson, former US Under Secretary of the Army, Robert O. Work, former US Deputy Secretary of Defense, Col. Woody Goldberg (Civilian Aide to Secretary of the Army), Dr. Gary Maita (Board Secretary, Bayonne Board of Education), Pam Itzkowitz (Superintendent, Baron Hirsch Cemetery), Marty Satloff (Senior Vice Commander of Jewish War Veterans, Post 80), Major John Quinn (Missouri National Guard), Paula Smith (Civilian Employee, Executive Communications, The Pentagon), Rachel Lithgow, (Past Executive Director, American Jewish Historical Society, NYC), Michael Perry (President and CEO, US Army Heritage and Educational Center, PA), Dr. Michael Bridgen (Emeritus Director and Professor of The Ranger School,

NY), Col. Paul Dietrich (Ret. Commander, Veterans of Foreign Wars and American Legion, S.I., NY), Lt. Col. (Ret.) Robert Wolff, Glen Flora (Ret. Commander, Veterans of Foreign Wars Post 226 Bayonne, NJ), Jackie George (Associate, Veterans of Foreign Wars, Post 226, Bayonne, NJ), David Laskin (Author, Seattle, WA), and John Conroy (Author and Journalist, Plattsburgh, NY).

About the Authors

Sara Shemin Cass is the eldest grandchild of Sgt. William Shemin. She has many life-shaping and important memories of him and experienced firsthand the importance he placed on patriotism, hard work, and family. She has worked at the Federal Reserve Bank of New York in Bank Supervision for over thirty-five years. A mother and grandmother, she was motivated to create this book to keep the legacy of William Shemin alive for the next generation of the Shemin family, as well as those too young to learn this story from those who had firsthand memories of the twentieth-century events described here.

Dan Burstein's grandmother, Leah Shemin Burstein, was William Shemin's first cousin. Dan's father, Leon Burstein, got his first job as a teenager working in Bill Shemin's greenhouse in the Bronx. Dan met Bill on several occasions, including once as a five-year-old when Bill told him stories from World War I. Dan is the author of fourteen nonfiction books, is managing partner of Millennium Technology Value Partners, a venture capital firm, and a father and grandfather. He traveled with his wife, Julie O'Connor, and son, David Burstein, on the 2018 family trip to the battlefields in France to mark the one hundredth anniversary of the battles in which both William Shemin and Henry Johnson fought.

About the Illustrator

Gary Bullock was born in northeast England, and after completing a Graphic Design Degree in Leeds and travelling abroad extensively, he finally settled in rural Shropshire. He has enjoyed a long career producing illustrations in a wide variety of styles (traditionally then digitally), for publishing, advertising, TV (Netflix), and info graphics (Mary Rose Museum) all from his home studio. Gary is renowned for adding that extra creative flair to all his commissions, whatever the project. Gary can be found at www.bullockillustration.com.

Photo Credits

LIBRARY OF CONGRESS

Pages: 27 (1917) Man buying *The Evening Star* from newsboy, Washington, D.C.—headline reads "U.S. at War with Germany". 1917. April 7. [Photograph] Retrieved from the Library of Congress, https://www.loc.gov/item/2001706358/.: 31 (top), Library of Congress, Music Division; 31 (bottom), Cammilli, E. (1917) The call to duty Join the Army for home and country. United States, 1917. [New York: Published by Recruiting Committee of the Mayor's Committee on National Defence [sic], N.Y.: American Lithographic Co] [Photograph] Retrieved from the Library of Congress, https://www.loc.gov/item/00651808/.; 36–37, King, W. L., King, W. L., photographer. (1919) No Man's Land, Flanders Field, France. Flanders France, 1919 [sic]. [Photograph] Retrieved from the Library of Congress, https://www.loc.gov/item/2007663169/; 39, Keystone View Company. (ca. 1918). "Over the top"—American soldiers answering the bugle call to "charge" (ca. 1918). Meadville, Pa.: Keystone View Co., March 25. [Photograph] Retrieved from the Library of Congress, https://www.loc.gov/item/96505415/.; 66, 302nd Eng. repairing road over trench and 92nd Div. colored machine gunners going into action, Argonne Forest, France. Argonne France, None. [Between 1917 and 1918] [Photograph] Retrieved from the Library of Congress, https://www.loc.gov/item/2017648704/.

THE NEW YORK TIMES

Page 29, *New York Times*, May 8, 1915. Page 30, *New York Times*, April 6, 1917.

THE NEW YORK PUBLIC LIBRARY

Page 47, Poster of Henry Johnson and Needham Roberts: New York Public Library/The Schomburg Center for Research in Black Culture/ Miles Vandahurst Lynk, 1919.

JULIE O'CONNOR

Pages: 6, 35 (bottom), 38, 49 (bottom), 54, 59 (top), 65, 69 (right), 81, 84, 86, 87, 88 (both photos), 89 (both photos), 90, 91, 92 (both photos), 93, and 100, Courtesy of Julie O'Connor.

SHEMIN FAMILY ARCHIVES

Pages: 2, 8, 11, 19, 20 (both photos), 21 (all three photos), 24, 26 (all three photos), 34 (both photos), 35 (top), 43, 50, 51, 52 (both photos), 53, 56, 57, 58, 59 (bottom), 60 (both photos), 61 (top), 62, 64, 67 (all photos), 68, 69 (left), 70, 71, 72, 76, 77, 82, 94, 95, 101 and 106, Courtesy of the Shemin Family Archives. Page 14: Pairing of Sgt. William Shemin's 4th Infantry Division's ivy insignia with an actual ivy cutting, by Evelyn Trichon and Elsie Shemin-Roth.

THE WEITZMAN NATIONAL MUSEUM OF AMERICAN JEWISH HISTORY

Pages: 16 (bottom), 78, Courtesy of the Weitzman National Museum of American Jewish History, 2018.24.1, Gift of Elsie Shemin-Roth and Ina Bass; 98–99, Courtesy of the Weitzman National Museum of American Jewish History, Photograph by Michael Christopher.

UNITED STATES ARMY

Pages: 10, 45 (top), 46, 49 (top), and 80, Courtesy of the United States Army. Photos on pages 16 (top), 45 (bottom), 83 and 108 are by Staff Sgt. Bernardo Fuller, United States Army, Courtesy of the United States Army.

Distinguished Figures in American Public Life Comment to Elsie Shemin-Roth on William Shemin's Heroism and *The Ivy Hero*

The book is very well done. William Shemin was a hero and an inspiration to us all with his dedication to his fellow soldiers and his country. It's great that his heroics, bravery, and leadership are finally recognized.

—US CONGRESSMAN BLAINE LUETKEMEYER *(R-MO)*

The Ivy Hero is inspiring!! Sgt. William Shemin's heroic battlefield actions exemplify our Soldier's Creed . . . Never Leave a Fallen Comrade. His greatest Legacy shines through generations . . . a Family of Servant Leaders who continue to strengthen our Communities and Inspire hope in the American Dream for which William Shemin and millions of fellow Veterans fought to perpetuate.

—GENERAL DAN ALLYN, *US Army (Retired)*

I couldn't be prouder that William Shemin and other Jewish heroes will get the recognition they deserve, and the national gratitude they earned.

—SENATOR CLAIRE MCCASKILL *(D-MO) at the time of William Shemin's Medal of Honor ceremony, 2015*

The Ivy Hero should be an inspiration for generations of adults and children for many years to come.

—RABBI JEFFREY STIFFMAN, *Senior Rabbi Emeritus, Congregation Shaare Emeth, St. Louis*

The Ivy Hero is a wonderful read and will provide its readership with insight into what true heroes are, and sacrifices they make for humanity.

—STEVE RUHNKE, *Retired Curator for the 4th Infantry Division Museum*

"The bravest man I ever knew," said our grandfather, Jim Pritchard, about his dear friend Bill Shemin. His heroic act saved our grandfather and allowed the creation of three more generations that now stretches across this country. The bond between the Shemin and Pritchard family is cherished and intertwined forever. *The Ivy Hero* book embodies the message of how one person's caring for his fellow man has a positive ripple effect on others that reverberates well into the future.

—LYNN PRITCHARD AND THE WHOLE PRITCHARD FAMILY *including 13 family members from three generations of descendants of their beloved hero, Sgt. Jim Pritchard, spread out through New York, New Jersey, Nebraska, Arizona, California.*

We are renaming a school for a hometown hero who went above and beyond. By dedicating this school, students will think about those who served and may well follow in his example to do what is right.

—JOHN NIESZ, *Bayonne, NJ Schools Superintendent, around the time of the ceremony naming one of Bayonne's schools The William Shemin Midtown Community School, 2019*

The book about your father came the other day, and I have really been enjoying it. I'm amazed at how well-preserved you and your family have kept your photos and history. I'm blown away by your family's selflessness at including Henry Johnson. It really shows the breadth of Medal of Honor recipients, both in terms of actions, backgrounds and what turns life took for both of them after the War. That your family ensured both stories continue to be told is an incredible service.

—MAJOR JOHN QUINN, *Missouri National Guard*

I received the advanced copy of *The Ivy Hero*. Many thanks for passing it along! The illustrations are great. I particularly like the early postwar photos, since they're so evocative of the era.

—PATRICK OSBORN *(Curator, National Archives)*

I wanted to drop a quick note to say thank you for the wonderful book about your father and Henry Johnson. It's an incredibly lovely tribute and you and your family should be very proud.

—MIKE VENSO, *Military and Firearms Curator, Missouri Historical Society, Soldiers Memorial Military Museum, St. Louis*

OMG! I am so impressed with the book. It is certainly something students can read and comprehend.

—PAT DZIUBEK, *Assistant Principal, Bayonne High School*

I received my copy of *The Ivy Hero* yesterday and I was overwhelmed with excitement. The book is absolutely fantastic. The writing is informative, and the pictures give it the extra visualization that brings the book to life. I am so honored to have been a part of this process and I can't thank you enough for bringing William Shemin into my life.

Your family is extraordinarily lucky to have this book to document William Shemin's life. I know that it was a labor of love and the result is simply wonderful. Generations will now know about William Shemin because of your prodigious effort.

> —TONYA ELISHA MELE *(Grade 6 English Language Arts Teacher, William Shemin Midtown Community School, Bayonne, NJ)*

Once I started to read *The Ivy Hero*, I couldn't put the book down. The book reveals how great William Shemin's efforts were for his country and his family.

> —BUDDY LEBMAN, *97 year-old World War II veteran, who saw action in the tank and artillery corps with General Patton and participated in the liberation of the Dachau concentration camp.*

The Ivy Hero is a truly inspirational accounting of a remarkable man whose courage, conviction and dedication are only eclipsed by his desire to serve and save his fellow man. Bill Shemin's sacrifice for his country is inspirational and uplifting and gives hope that his life will inspire the next generation that is called to serve above and beyond. Love of country and love of fellow man are echoed through this wonderful book. No one who reads about Bill can help but feel motivated to act courageously not only under fire but in every day decisions that confront us all.

> —JACK PIROZZI, *former Executive Director, major gifts program, Washington University, St. Louis*

On *The Ivy Hero:* 'Tis a real treasure!

> —COL. SHERWOOD (WOODY) GOLDBERG
> *(Civilian Aide to the Secretary of the Army)*

I got *The Ivy Hero* yesterday. It is great. My family loves it. It is my new history book. I am a visual person and I really love the old pictures. I have been showing it off. So, thank you, thank you. And thank you for including the story of Henry Johnson.

—COMMAND SERGEANT MAJOR (RET.) LOUIS WILSON

I just got your early reader's release of *The Ivy Hero* book and must say, it is terrific!

—COL. RICHARD GOLDENBERG, *US Army
National Guard*

The Ivy Hero is wonderful. I'm going to see about having the book added to our Hall of Honor display, where we recognize William. Really good stuff!

—MIKE HAYNIE, *Vice Chancellor, Syracuse University
& Executive Director, D'Aniello Institute for Veterans
and Military Families (IVMF)*

The Ivy Hero book helped me develop a better understanding of Bill Shemin after his war experiences. It is a well-written biography, and very appropriate for young readers. It also describes the family's efforts, especially those of Elsie, to correct a flaw of the United States government.

—DR. MICHAEL BRIDGEN, *Emeritus Director and
Professor of The Ranger School, NY*

**For more information about this book visit the website
www.TheIvyHero.com**